THE
CHRISTIAN
FOCUS
STORY
BIBLE

THE CHRISTIAN FOCUS STORY BIBLE

Carine Mackenzie

Illustrated by Kevin Kimber

CF4•K

© Copyright 2004 Carine Mackenzie
Reprinted in 2009, ISBN 978-1-84550-494-6

First published in 2004, ISBN 978-1-85792-851-8
by Christian Focus Publications
Geanies House, Fearn, Ross-shire, IV20 1TW
Scotland, U.K.
www.christianfocus.com
Illustrations by Kevin Kimber
Cover design by Daniel van Straaten
Printed in China

Given with love to

_____

on

_____

by

_____

Contents

1. God Made the World 8

2. God Made Adam and Eve 10

3. Safe in the Ark 12

4. Abraham – The Friend of God 14

5. Isaac - The Promised Son 16

6. Isaac and Rebekah 18

7. Jacob and Esau 20

8. Joseph – The Dreamer 22

9. Joseph in Egypt 24

10. Jochabed's Baby 26

11. Moses and the Burning Bush 28

12. Plagues and Passover 30

13. Crossing the Red Sea 32

14. In the Wilderness 34

15. The Ten Commandments 36

16. Spies and a Bronze Serpent...................... 38

17. Two Spies and a Red Rope 40

18. Gideon's Sword 42

19. Love at Harvest Time 44

20. Samuel the Servant 46

21. David the Shepherd 48

22. David and Jonathan 50

23. Solomon the Wise 52

24. Elijah the Prophet 54

25. Elisha and Naaman 56

26. Joash The Boy King 58

27. Nehemiah - God's Builder 60

28. Esther the Queen...................... 62

29. A Very Patient Man...................... 64

30. The Fiery Furnace 66

31. Daniel and the Lions 68

32. Jonah and the Big Fish 70

33. John the Baptist 72

34. The Birth of Jesus 74

35. Shepherds, Simeon and Anna 76

36. The Wise Men and their Gifts................ 78

37. The Boy Jesus 80

38. The Baptism of Jesus 82

39. Jesus is Tempted by Satan 84

40. The Twelve Disciples 86

41. The Miracle at the Wedding 88

42. The Woman at the Well 90

43. The Sower's Story 92

44. The Builders' Story 94

45. Calming the Storm 96

46. Jesus Feeds a Huge Crowd 98

47. Jairus' Daughter is Healed 100

48. Jesus Teaches on a Mountain 102

49. Martha and Mary 104

50. Lazarus 106

51. Zacchaeus 108

52. A Lost Sheep and a Lost Coin 110

53. Jesus Heals a Blind Man 112

54. The Kind Man 114

55. The Good Shepherd 116

56. The Tax Collector's Prayer 118

57. To Jerusalem 120

58. The Last Supper 122

59. In the Garden of Gethsemane 124

60. Peter Denies Jesus 126

61. Jesus Dies 128

62. Jesus Lives Again 130

63. Picnic on the Shore 132

64. Jesus Goes Back to Heaven 134

65. The Day of Pentecost 136

66. Stephen the Martyr 138

67. The Miracle on the Road 140

68. Dorcas and her Sewing Basket 142

69. Paul the Missionary 144

70. Paul Travels Again 146

71. The Philippian Jailer 148

72. Paul's Long Sermon 150

73. Journey to Rome 152

74. Letters to the Churches 154

75. The Prisoner at Patmos 156

1. GOD MADE THE WORLD

(GENESIS 1)

In the beginning God made the whole world from nothing. On the first day God said, "Let there be light," and light appeared. God saw that the light was good. God called the light *day* and he called the darkness *night*.

On the second day God made the sky with all the different clouds. All the water was made by God - oceans, seas, rivers, lakes. On the third day, God said, "Let dry ground appear." And so the hills and valleys, mountains and plains were formed. By his powerful Word God made the trees and plants, bushes and flowers. God saw that all he had made was good.

On the fourth day God made the sun and moon and stars which we see in the sky. On the fifth day God made the fish and sea creatures which live in the oceans and the beautiful birds which can fly through the air.

On the sixth day God made all the animals. "Let the land produce living creatures," he said. And so all sorts of wonderful animals came into being – the giraffe, the cow, the mouse and the firefly. Everything was good.

God saw that all he had made was good.

God is the Creator

God made the world out of nothing. To make a cake, we need eggs, flour and sugar. To make a picture, we need paper and paints. God made the world out of nothing. He spoke the word and it was done. Isn't that amazing?

2. GOD MADE ADAM AND EVE

(GENESIS 1–3)

On day six God made a man called Adam from the dust of the ground. He breathed life into him. God did not want Adam to be alone so he made him fall asleep. He then removed one of his ribs and from this he made a woman. Adam was very glad.

Adam and Eve were different to animals. God gave them a living soul. He blessed them and told them to have children. They ruled over all the other animals in the garden. God saw that everything was good and rested on the seventh day. It was a day of rest for man too.

God told Adam that he was not allowed to eat from the tree of knowledge of good and evil. But Satan, disguised as a serpent, tempted Eve. Eve listened to Satan's lie and ate the fruit. She gave some to Adam too. Sin spoiled God's creation. Adam and Eve knew they had disobeyed God and tried to hide from him. "Where are you, Adam?" God called out. Adam could not hide any longer. He blamed Eve and Eve blamed the serpent. God had to punish sin. Hardship, pain and death entered the world that day.

God gave Adam and Eve a garden to live in.

Jesus is the Saviour

Jesus died to save us from our sins. Adam and Eve's children were born sinners. When they grew up Cain killed Abel, his brother. Sin affects our lives too, but because of what Jesus has done we can trust in him to save us from sin.

3. SAFE IN THE ARK

(GENESIS 6–9)

People on the earth became more evil. God sent a big flood to destroy them. Noah, who was a good man, was warned by God about the flood. God told Noah to build a big boat – and he told him how big to make it. Noah, his wife, his sons Shem, Ham and Japheth and their wives, were all to go into the big boat – the ark. Two of every animal (and seven of some) were also taken into the ark.

Then God shut the doors and the rain began to fall. It rained for forty days and nights. The earth was flooded. The bad people were destroyed. The waters covered the earth for 150 days. At last the ark came to rest on top of Mount Ararat. Noah sent out a raven and a dove. The raven did not come back as it found food elsewhere, but the dove returned. It could find no place to rest. Seven days later the dove was sent out again. This time it brought back an olive leaf. Noah knew that the trees must be visible. Seven days later the dove did not return. Noah knew the land was dry. Noah and his family thanked God for saving them. God promised that he would never again flood the whole earth. He put the rainbow in the sky as a sign of his promise.

The rainbow is the sign of God's promise.

God is Great

God wants to bless you. Noah obeyed God's Word and was saved from the flood. How can we obey God? How does God bless us and save us today? God has blessed us by giving us his Word and telling us about his Son.

4. ABRAHAM – THE FRIEND OF GOD

(GENESIS 12–15)

Abraham and his wife Sarah lived in the land of Mesopotamia. He was rich, and owned many sheep, cows, donkeys and camels. Sarah was very beautiful, but they had no children.

God told Abraham to leave his house and travel a long distance to another land. God promised to guide him. Abraham and Sarah set out on their long journey, obeying God's commands. God made a special promise (or covenant) to Abraham. "I will make your family into a great nation. I will bless you." This was amazing news when Sarah and Abraham had no child and were growing old.

When they reached Canaan, God told Abraham that this was the land that he had promised to give him and his children. But the herdsmen of Lot, Abraham's nephew, began to quarrel with Abraham's herdsmen about the pasture land for their animals. Wisely Abraham suggested to Lot that they settle in different parts of the country to avoid trouble.

Lot chose the fertile plains of Jordan to the east and Abraham went in the other direction. Abraham worshipped God and was known as a friend of God.

God told Abraham to travel to another land.

God is our Friend

Abraham was a friend of God. Think about one of your friends. Why are you friends? You talk and spend time together. You listen to them and you love them. Are you a friend of God?

5. ISAAC - THE PROMISED SON

(GENESIS 16–22)

God promised Abraham a son. As Sarah grew older she became impatient, but God reminded Abraham that Sarah would have a son – just as he had promised.

One day Abraham was at the door of the tent when three visitors arrived. He welcomed them and gave them a good meal. They were God's messengers. "This time next year," they said, "Sarah will have a son." Sarah overheard and laughed out loud. God rebuked her, "Is anything too hard for the Lord?" It wasn't! Isaac was born when Abraham was one hundred years old and Sarah ninety. Abraham believed God's promise, but his faith was put to the test. "Take Isaac to Mount Moriah," God said, "and sacrifice him there as an offering to me." Abraham still believed in God. So early in the morning he and Isaac climbed Mount Moriah.

Abraham built an altar and placed Isaac on it. He raised the knife to kill him. The angel of the Lord called out "Abraham, Abraham! Do not harm the boy. I know you fear God for you were willing to sacrifice your son." Abraham then saw a ram caught in a bush. This was used as a sacrifice instead.

God gave Abraham a son.

God is Welcoming

God loves you. God's son, the Lord Jesus, was sacrificed for sin.
God gave his son for us. He promises his people that "the one
who comes to me I will never cast out."

6. ISAAC AND REBEKAH

(GENESIS 24–25)

Abraham wanted Isaac to marry a girl from Mesopotamia. He sent a trusted servant to find her. The servant prayed that God would guide him to the right girl. When he arrived in the city of Nahor he went to the local well. A young woman named Rebekah was there. She gave the servant a refreshing drink of water and even offered to give his thirsty camels water to drink. This meant lifting out lots of heavy water from the well, but she did this without complaint.

Abraham's servant believed God had guided him to this girl. She was pretty, hard working and from the right family. Rebekah's parents agreed to let her marry Abraham's son. It would be a long journey for Rebekah and she would have to leave her home and family, but her parents agreed and Rebekah did too. Isaac and Rebekah were married when Isaac was forty years old. However, twenty years later they still had no children. Isaac prayed to God for a child. God heard him and soon they had twin boys. God was keeping his promise made to Abraham years before. Abraham's grandchildren were now born.

Rebekah went to collect water at the well.

God is Caring

Rebekah had to collect water for the household. Water is very important. We should thank God for it. How often do you use water during a normal day?

7. JACOB AND ESAU

(GENESIS 25–27)

Rebekah's boys didn't even look alike. Esau, the eldest was red and hairy and loved the outdoor life. Jacob was smooth skinned and preferred a quiet life at home. Esau had the birthright to be the head of the family and a bigger share of his father's property. However, one day he came home from hunting, very hungry. "Give me some stew," Esau asked Jacob. "I am faint with hunger."

"I'll give you some, if you give me your birthright," replied Jacob.

"What is the use of a birthright to me, if I die of hunger?" said Esau.

So Esau got his stew and Jacob got the birthright. Then one day Isaac wanted to ask God to bless Esau. Rebekah overheard old blind Isaac's plans. He told Esau to hunt for venison, so Rebekah ran off to make some goat stew which tasted like venison. Jacob then dressed in Esau's clothes and put goatskins on. He smelt and felt like Esau. Isaac was tricked into praying with Jacob instead of Esau. Isaac asked God to make Jacob prosperous. Esau was so angry when he came home. He had lost the birthright and the blessing.

Esau came home. He was very hungry.

God is Right

Should Esau have sold his birthright for a plate of stew? Was Jacob right to deceive his father with the goat's hair in order to gain a blessing? We should always follow God. His Word is true and right.

8. JOSEPH – THE DREAMER

(GENESIS 37)

Jacob became the father of twelve boys and one girl. To his favourite son Joseph he gave a beautiful coat. This made the other brothers jealous. They became angry when Joseph told them about a dream he had. "We were all in a field tying up corn. My sheaf stood up straight and yours all bowed down to mine." Joseph then told them another dream. "The sun, moon and eleven stars bowed down to me." The brothers were even more envious.

One day Jacob sent Joseph out to visit his brothers who were looking after the sheep. When the brothers saw Joseph coming they plotted together. "Let's kill him," one said, "and throw his body in a pit." "No," said Reuben. "Don't harm him. Just throw him in the pit." So they tore off his lovely coloured coat and threw him in the pit. Reuben planned to rescue him later, but while he was elsewhere the others sold Joseph for twenty pieces of silver to a group of merchants on their way to Egypt.

They dipped Joseph's coat in goat's blood and showed it to Jacob. He was heart broken, believing that his son was dead.

Jacob gave Joseph a coat of many colours.

Jesus is Sinless

Jesus is sinless, but we aren't. In this story one sin led to another. Jealousy lead to hatred, then cruelty and lying. God says that all have sinned. Ask God to forgive your sins in Jesus' name.

9. JOSEPH IN EGYPT

(GENESIS 39–46)

Joseph was sold to an important man called Potiphar. God helped Joseph in this difficult situation. He worked well. His master trusted him. But Potiphar's wife accused Joseph of something he had not done. Potiphar believed his wife and Joseph was thrown into prison. However, God was with Joseph in prison too. Soon the prison guards were trusting Joseph with special duties.

With God's help he explained a dream to Pharaoh's butler. But when the butler was back working in the palace he forgot all about Joseph. Then one night Pharaoh had bad dreams. No one could tell the meaning. Joseph was summoned to the palace. God told him what the dream meant and Joseph was put in charge of the storage of food crops which would feed the people during the expected famine. Then Joseph's brothers arrived in Egypt wanting to buy food. They fell down before Joseph begging for food, not realising who he was. After testing them several times Joseph told them who he was. "Don't be grieved," he said. "God has sent me here to preserve life."

Jacob was joyfully reunited with his son Joseph.

God was with Joseph in prison.

God is in Control

God helped Joseph. Joseph's brothers meant to harm him, but in actual fact this was all part of God's plan to help Joseph's own family in the future famine.

10. JOCHABED'S BABY

(EXODUS 1–2)

Many years later another Pharaoh ruled Egypt. He hated the Israelites. He made them slaves and threw their baby boys into the River Nile. However, one little boy survived. He was born to Amram and his wife Jochabed. They hid the baby in the house for three months, but when they couldn't do that any longer Jochabed made a waterproof basket out of bulrushes and put the baby in it. She took the basket to the river and floated it at the water's edge.

The baby's sister Miriam watched from close by and saw Pharaoh's daughter come down to the river to bathe. The princess saw the basket and asked for it to be brought to her. When she saw the baby he started to cry. Miriam came to speak to the princess. "Shall I go and fetch a nurse for you?" she asked. The princess agreed.

Miriam ran for her mother. Jochabed could now look after her baby openly. The princess called him Moses. When Moses was older he went to live at the palace as the adopted son of Pharaoh's daughter. But he never forgot that he belonged to the people of God.

She put the baby in a basket in the river.

God is Faithful

Moses' mother and father had great faith in God. They trusted him with the life of their little baby. We should trust God too. We can trust him to save us from our sins through the death of his Son, Jesus Christ.

11. MOSES AND THE BURNING BUSH

(EXODUS 3–4)

When Moses was older he ran away from Egypt to Midian. Pharaoh was angry with him and Moses was afraid for his life. In Midian he married a woman named Zipporah, but back in Egypt things were even worse for the Israelite people. However, God had a plan to save them. One day Moses was looking after his sheep. He noticed a bush burning fiercely, but not burning up and went over to look more closely. God spoke to Moses from the burning bush, "Moses, Moses."

"Here I am," replied Moses.

"Take your sandals off," said God, "for where you are standing is holy ground."

God told Moses to go to Pharaoh and ask him to let God's people go. God promised to be with Moses and bring them to a good land. Moses was not sure, so God showed his power by turning Moses' rod into a serpent then back to a rod. Moses still wasn't sure. "I won't know what to say," he exclaimed.

"I will teach you what to say," said God, "Aaron your brother will help you."

Moses then returned to Egypt to face Pharaoh.

God spoke to Moses from the burning bush.

God is With Us

When Moses was anxious and unsure God said to him, "I will be with you." He has promised to be with us too.

12. PLAGUES AND PASSOVER

(EXODUS 4–12)

Moses and Aaron went to see Pharaoh. "God says, 'Let my people go.'"

Pharaoh would not allow it. So God sent ten different plagues to Egypt to teach Pharaoh about God's power.

First the River Nile was turned to blood. The fish died. No one could drink from the river. Still Pharaoh refused to listen to God. Next came a plague of frogs – in the palace, in the house, even in the beds, the ovens and the baking bowls. "Get rid of the frogs and I'll let the people go," promised Pharaoh. But he went back on his word when the frogs went.

Then came lice, flies, cattle disease, boils, hailstones, locusts and darkness. Still Pharaoh was stubborn. The tenth plague was worst of all – the first born in every Egyptian family died. There was great sadness in Egypt, but the first born of the Israelite people were saved. They had been told by God to put lambs' blood on the doors of their houses. When the angel of death saw the blood he would "pass over" that house. The families ate a feast that night of the lamb roasted. This feast was called the Passover Feast.

Every family had a feast.

Jesus is the Bread of Life

The Israelites had the Passover Feast to remind them of how God rescued them from Egypt. Jesus' followers also have a special meal. It is called the Lord's Supper and reminds them of how Jesus died to rescue them from sin.

13. CROSSING THE RED SEA

(EXODUS 13–15)

After the tenth plague Pharaoh begged the Israelites to leave. So God's people left Egypt on foot to the land God had promised them. As they went God guided them with a pillar of cloud by day and a pillar of fire by night.

When Pharaoh realised that all his slaves had left, he changed his mind again. He sent chariots and soldiers to bring them back. The Israelites were scared when they realised that Pharaoh's army was after them and the Red Sea was in front. "Why did you bring us out here to die?" they complained to Moses.

"Stand still and see the salvation of the Lord," he replied. "The Lord will fight for you." Moses stretched out his hand and the Lord parted the waters by a strong east wind. God had made a path for them right through the middle and so the Israelites walked across on dry land. They saw God's great power and believed in him. However, Pharaoh's army rushed towards the towering waters too. But when they were on the sea bed God made their chariot wheels come off. Moses stretched out his hand and the water flowed back as before. All the Egyptian army were drowned. God's people were safe.

God made a path through the sea.

Jesus is the Redeemer

When we trust Jesus he frees us or redeems us from sin. The Israelites were freed from slavery. Jesus saves us from being slaves to sin. We want to please God instead of doing wrong.

14. IN THE WILDERNESS

(EXODUS 15–17)

God looked after the Israelite people as they journeyed through the wilderness. However, after a few weeks they began to complain. There was not much to eat. They longed for the food they had in Egypt. However, they shouldn't have complained because God provided for all their needs.

He sent small birds called quail to the camp in the evening and each morning the ground was covered with small pieces of a strange white substance. The people wondered what it was and said to each other "Manna," meaning "What is it?" So that's how it got its name. This manna was bread from heaven and tasted like honey wafers. Each family gathered enough for their daily needs, but on the sixth day they had to gather enough for the Sabbath day also.

One day the Israelites needed water and God provided that too. Moses struck a rock with his rod and more than enough water poured out. God provided for all their needs for many, many, years. In fact God provided the manna for forty years. He made sure that his people had enough to eat and drink until they had settled in the land he had promised.

Each family took the food that they needed.

God is Generous

God gave the Israelites what they needed. He gives us what we need too. We should pray to God and ask him for our daily bread. Remember to thank him every time you eat and drink.

15. THE TEN COMMANDMENTS

(EXODUS 19–20)

Three months after they left Egypt, God's people reached Sinai. Then God spoke to Moses. He said, "Tell the people, 'If you obey me and keep my covenant you will be a special treasure to me.'"

"All that the Lord has spoken we will do," they promised. On Mount Sinai God gave them laws about how to worship God and how to live. God gave Moses two stones with the Ten Commandments written on them by God himself. These Commandments are:

1.   You shall not worship any other God but me.

2.   You shall not make any idol.

3.   You shall not speak God's name in vain.

4.   Keep the Sabbath day holy.

5.   Honour your father and mother.

6.   You shall not murder.

7.   You shall not commit adultery.

8.   You shall not steal.

9.   You shall not bear false witness.

10.   You shall not covet someone else's belongings.

All that the Lord has spoken we will do.

God is Love

God is love. We should love God and our neighbour. This is what Jesus said and Jesus kept God's commands perfectly.

16. SPIES AND A BRONZE SERPENT

(NUMBERS 21)

God told Moses to send out twelve men to spy on the Promised Land. Huge bunches of grapes were brought back which showed that the land was fertile. However, ten spies complained that the people were like giants and that the cities had big strong walls. They didn't want to attack. Two other spies disagreed. Caleb and Joshua trusted in God. "Do not rebel against God," they urged. "The Lord is with us. Do not be afraid."

But the people didn't listen and many rebelled against God. So God did not allow them to see the promised land. Joshua and Caleb who trusted God, were among those who finally did reach the promised land of Canaan many years later. Meanwhile, the people often complained against God. One day God punished them by sending fierce serpents to the camp. Many were bitten and died. "We have sinned against God," the people said to Moses, "Please pray that God would take the serpents away." Moses did this and then God told him what to do. "Make a bronze serpent," he said, "and put it up on a pole. When someone has been bitten, he only has to look at this serpent and he will live."

God told Moses what to do.

Jesus is the Healer

In John chapter 3 verse 14 Jesus compared himself to the bronze serpent that was lifted up. Jesus was lifted up to die on a cross. He heals us from sin if we look to him for forgiveness.

17. TWO SPIES AND A RED ROPE

(JOSHUA 1–6)

Joshua led the Israelites after Moses died. "Be strong and courageous," God told him. "I am with you wherever you go." One day Joshua sent two spies to the city of Jericho. A woman named Rahab hid them on her roof when the soldiers came. Rahab knew that the Lord God was the one true God. The spies promised to be kind to her when the Israelites attacked. Rahab then helped them escape down a red rope tied to her window. "Tie this rope in the window," the spies told her. "When our soldiers see it you and your family will be safe."

When the spies returned to Joshua they had good news to report.

"The Lord will give us the land," they exclaimed.

God told Joshua what to do. The Israelite soldiers marched round the city once for six days. Seven priests blew ram's horns. On the seventh day they marched round seven times. The priests blew the trumpets, everyone gave a loud shout, then the walls fell down. Just as God promised. And just as the spies had promised Rahab and her family were saved.

Rahab helped the spies escape.

Jesus is the Life

God's people are saved from sin. The name Joshua means *the Lord saves*. The name Jesus means *Saviour*. Because of his death on the cross Jesus saved his people from their sins.

18. GIDEON'S SWORD

(JUDGES 6–8)

The Midianites were stealing Israel's crops and animals. God sent an angel to speak to a man named Gideon. The angel told Gideon that God had chosen him to save his people. So Gideon built an altar to worship God and he destroyed the altars to the false god, Baal. Then Gideon planned to fight the mighty Midianite army with his big army of 32,000 soldiers. However, God told Gideon to make his army smaller so that they would not boast that they had won by their own strength.

Any soldier who was afraid was allowed to go home and then at the river just those who drank water from their hands were allowed to stay. This meant that there were only 300 soldiers left. Gideon prayed and then the 300 men were divided into three groups. Each soldier had a trumpet and a burning flame covered by a jar. When Gideon blew his trumpet, they all blew their trumpets, smashed their jars and shouted, "The sword of the Lord and of Gideon!"

The enemy soldiers were terrified and confused. They started fighting with each other and ran away. God had saved the Israelites using Gideon and a very small army.

God told Gideon to make his army smaller.

God is to be Worshipped

Gideon built an altar to worship God. We can worship God in church, when we pray, sing praises, or read God's Word. We can also worship God by obeying him.

19. LOVE AT HARVEST TIME

(RUTH 1–4)

There was a famine in Israel, so a man named Elimelech, his wife Naomi and their two sons travelled from Bethlehem to the land of Moab where there was plenty of food. Elimelech died there. When Naomi's sons grew up they married Moabite girls – Orpah and Ruth. But when both sons died Orpah, Ruth and Naomi were all widows with no men to provide for them. Naomi decided to go back to Bethlehem. Orpah remained in Moab, but Ruth insisted on going with Naomi. "Where you go, I will go and where you stay I will stay: Your people will be my people and your God my God."

When they arrived in Bethlehem it was harvest time and Ruth went to work in the fields. God guided her to a field belonging to Boaz who was very good to her. "I know how kind you are to Naomi," he told her, "and how you have come to trust in the Lord God."

Naomi was pleased to hear how Ruth had met Boaz. He was a relative of her husband. By law he could buy back or redeem the family land and marry Ruth. Boaz was delighted to do this. Eventually God gave them a baby son, Obed, and Naomi was happy again.

Your God will be my God.

God is a Rewarder

God loves to bless his people. Ruth followed God. God blessed her life and rewarded her for her kindness to Naomi.

20. SAMUEL THE SERVANT

(SAMUEL 1–3)

Hannah had no children. She prayed to God for a child. God answered her and soon she had a baby son. He was called Samuel, which means "asked of God". When he was older Hannah took him to live at the temple where he would serve God. Every year she made him a new coat and went to visit him.

One evening after finishing his work, Samuel went to bed. He suddenly heard a voice calling his name "Samuel!" He ran through to Eli the priest to ask him what he wanted. "I did not call you," said Eli. "Go back to bed."

This happened three times. Eli then realised that God was calling Samuel. He told Samuel what to say. When God spoke again, Samuel said, "Speak, Lord, for your servant is listening." God told him he would judge Eli's family because his sons were living sinful lives and Eli had not stopped them. Eli's sons were killed in battle. When Eli heard the bad news he fell back in shock and died too. Samuel grew up to be an important man of God – a prophet and priest teaching God's Word.

Speak, Lord, for your servant is listening.

God is our Help

You can tell God about your problems and ask him to help. Samuel listened to God. God speaks to us in the Bible. We should listen to what he says to us there.

21. DAVID THE SHEPHERD

(SAMUEL 16–17)

David was Jesse's youngest son. He looked after the sheep and protected them from lions and bears. One day David came home to meet an important visitor. Samuel the prophet had met all of Jesse's other sons, but still was not satisfied. When David came in, God told Samuel, "This is the one. Anoint him as king." Samuel poured the anointing oil over David's head. God had chosen him to be King of Israel. God would now be with David in a powerful way.

One day David went to visit his older brothers who were soldiers for King Saul. They were fighting the Philistines. David discovered that the Philistine's champion soldier was Goliath. He was over three metres tall. But when David heard Goliath shouting insults, he could not understand why no one fought him so he offered to do it himself. "God will help me. He helped me fight a lion and a bear."

He chose five smooth stones and placed one firmly within his slingshot. He then quickly threw his arm forward and let the stone fly through the air. The stone struck Goliath – smack – right in the middle of the forehead and he fell down dead. The Philistines ran for their lives, pursued by Saul's army. David was a hero.

God will help me. He helped me fight a lion.

God is our Strength

David trusted in God even when facing the terrifying Goliath.
You can trust in God too when you have problems.

22. DAVID AND JONATHAN

(SAMUEL 18–20)

King Saul became jealous of David because he was so popular – he even tried to kill him, but God kept David safe. Jonathan, Saul's son, was a good friend to David and when David wondered if it was safe to visit the palace, Jonathan promised to find out and give a signal to David.

When Jonathan spoke with his father he realised that Saul would kill David if he got a chance. So Jonathan went out to shoot arrows with a servant boy near where David was hiding. He shot an arrow far in the distance and shouted to the boy, "The arrow is beyond you." David heard this and knew that Jonathan was telling him that he had better go away.

Although Jonathan was the king's son and might have expected to be king himself one day, he knew that David was God's choice to rule Israel and he was not jealous. Then, when Jonathan and Saul both died in a battle with the Philistines, David finally became king. But he did not forget Jonathan and showed great kindness to Jonathan's son, Mephibosheth. Because he was Jonathan's son he was invited to eat at the table of King David every day.

David was God's choice for king.

God is the Best

We can be friends with God. Jonathan was a loyal friend to David. Jesus tells us to love our neighbour as ourselves. How can you show friendship to others?

23. SOLOMON THE WISE

(1 KINGS 2–10)

Solomon ruled Israel after his father David. He asked God for an understanding heart so that he would have wisdom to judge the people. God did this and gave him riches and honour too.

Solomon showed his wisdom when two women came to see him. Both claimed to be the mother of the same baby. "We live in the same house," explained one woman. "Her child died in the night so she stole my baby while I slept." The other woman denied this, "No the baby is mine." How would Solomon solve this problem? "Bring me a sword," he ordered. "We will divide the child in two and give you half each."

"Oh no," cried the first woman. "Do not kill him, give her the baby." Solomon knew she was the real mother and gave her the child.

Solomon was famous for his wisdom. Even the Queen of Sheba came to see for herself if the reports were true. She asked many questions and Solomon was able to explain everything. She was amazed at the splendour of Solomon's household. "The half was not told me," she said. The two rulers exchanged presents before the Queen of Sheba returned home.

He asked God for an understanding heart.

God is Wise

God can make us wise too. The Queen of Sheba went to great trouble to find King Solomon. Jesus is greater and wiser than Solomon. How do we find out more about Him? In God's Word, the Bible.

24. ELIJAH THE PROPHET

(1 KINGS 17)

Elijah was a prophet who spoke God's Word to the people of Israel. God told him to tell King Ahab that there would be no rain or dew in Israel for a long time. After Elijah gave this message, he hid by the brook Cherith where there was still water to drink. God provided for his needs and sent ravens with bread and meat every morning and evening.

When the brook dried up God told Elijah to go to Zarephath. A widow and her son were there. They shared the last of their food with Elijah. God then did a wonderful miracle. Until the rains came back their barrel of meal and their jug of oil did not go empty. But one day the widow's son tragically died. She was very upset. Elijah took the boy upstairs and laid him on a bed. He stretched himself on top of the boy's body three times and prayed.

God heard his prayer and restored the boy to life. Elijah brought him back downstairs to his mother. "Now I know that you are a man of God," she said, "and that the word of the Lord that you speak is the truth."

God sent ravens with bread and meat.

God is our Provider

God provided food for Elijah in difficult times. God provides our food for us. Look up Matthew chapter 6 verse 11 where Jesus tells us how to pray for our food every day.

25. ELISHA AND NAAMAN

(2 KINGS 5)

Naaman was a commander in the Syrian army. He was brave and important, but had a big problem. He suffered from a terrible skin disease called leprosy. A servant girl, from Israel, who was a slave in Naaman's house had an idea about how he could be healed. "If only he could see the prophet Elisha in Samaria," she told Naaman's wife. "He could heal him of his leprosy."

Naaman heard this and arranged to travel to Samaria. When he arrived at Elisha's house, Elisha did not come out to greet him. Instead he sent out a messenger to tell him to wash in the River Jordan seven times. Naaman was furious. "Are not the rivers of Damascus far better than any river in Israel?" he raged.

His servants persuaded him to think again, "If the prophet had told you to do something difficult would you not have done it? Why not do what he says? Wash and be clean." So Naaman dipped in the River Jordan seven times and his leprosy was cured. When he went back to Elisha's house he said to him, "The God of Israel is the only true God."

A little servant girl worked in Naaman's house.

Jesus is the Deliverer

Naaman was cleansed from leprosy by washing in the Jordan. God's people are cleansed from sin by Jesus Christ. "Wash me and I shall be whiter than the snow," Psalm 51 verse 7.

26. JOASH THE BOY KING

(2 CHRONICLES 22–23)

Joash was the son of Ahaziah King of Judah. Ahaziah did not love God and was killed when Joash was just a baby. When Athaliah, Joash's grandmother heard that Ahaziah was dead, she decided to kill all the royal family and make herself queen. However, Joash's aunt, Jehosheba, secretly hid Joash in the temple where she and her husband Jehoida, the priest, looked after Joash for six years.

During that time Jehoiada made a plan to put Joash on the throne. He sent for the commanders of the army and asked them to stand guard with all their men at the temple. Jehoida brought seven-year-old Joash out of the temple, put the crown on his head and proclaimed him king. He was anointed with oil, the people clapped their hands and shouted, "Long live the King."

When Athaliah heard the noise she hurried to the temple and saw the newly crowned Joash. "Treason! Treason!" she screamed, but the soldiers seized her and put her to death.

Joash was king in Judah for forty years and he was a good king when he had Jehoida the priest to help him.

The people shouted, "Long live the King!"

God is our Teacher

When Joash listened to Jehoida's advice he was a good king.
We should listen to godly advice from those who love God, but
the best advice comes from God himself (2 Timothy 3:15).

27. NEHEMIAH - GOD'S BUILDER

(NEHEMIAH 1–9)

Nehemiah was living in far-off Persia. His job was to serve wine to the King. But when he heard that the walls of his home city, Jerusalem, had been broken down he prayed to God for help. Nehemiah was very sad. When the King saw him he asked, "What's troubling you?"

"The city of my family is in ruins and the walls are burned down," he replied.

"What do you want?" asked the King.

Nehemiah quickly prayed and then asked the King if he could go to Jerusalem to rebuild the walls. The King agreed. When Nehemiah arrived in Jerusalem he went and looked at all the damage. A lot of work had to be done. Many people wanted to help him, but some tried to stop him. They said that the work was useless. However, Nehemiah trusted God and prayed for help. Soon the wall was half finished. A man called Sanballet and his wicked friends planned to destroy it,

 but Nehemiah kept on praying. He told the builders to carry a sword in one hand and work with the other. With God's help the wall of Jerusalem was rebuilt in just fifty-two days.

Nehemiah prayed to God and asked for help.

God is the Hearer of Prayer

Many Israelites were taken away from their homes and forced to live in the land of Persia. Nehemiah did not forget God and his laws when he was there. He prayed to God.

28. ESTHER THE QUEEN

(ESTHER 1–10)

Esther was a beautiful Jewish girl brought up in Persia by her cousin Mordecai. One day, King Ahasurerus, chose Esther as his new queen. She did not say she was Jewish, which was just as well, because Haman, the king's servant, hated the Jews and planned to kill them all. Mordecai begged Esther to ask the king for help. "Who knows if you have become queen for this reason," he told her.

Esther took a big risk and went to see the king uninvited, but he was pleased to see her. Esther asked him and Haman to a banquet. This made Haman very smug. He built some gallows to hang Mordecai on, but his plan backfired. The king heard of how Mordecai had once saved his life. Haman then had to lead Mordecai round the city on a royal horse, wearing a crown and robes.

But Haman went to Esther's banquet which pleased him. He actually went to two. At the second banquet Esther put her plan into action. She begged the king to save her people from Haman's wicked plot. The king was so angry he hanged Hamaan on the gallows that had been built for Mordecai. Mordecai was promoted and Haman's law was reversed. God had saved his people.

Ask the King for help.

God is the Answerer of Prayer

Esther took a risk when she went to the king without an invitation. We can speak to God at any time. We do not need to be afraid.

29. A VERY PATIENT MAN

(JOB CHAPTERS 1–42)

Job lived in the land of Uz. He had 7000 sheep, 3000 camels, 500 pairs of oxen, 500 donkeys and a large house. Job worshipped God and God was pleased with him. But one day, Satan, the evil one, said to God, "Job is only good because he has an easy life. Take away his possessions and he will curse you."

So God allowed Satan to test Job's faith by attacking his possessions. His animals were stolen or destroyed. His children were all killed. But Job still worshipped God and said, "The Lord gave and the Lord has taken away. Blessed be the name of the Lord." When Job's body was covered with boils he was so patient. "We accept good from God; should we not also accept hardship." Job's friends were no comfort. One said that he deserved his suffering. However, Job still trusted God and said, "I know that my redeemer lives."

When God spoke to him, Job understood God's power. He turned away from his sins and prayed for his friends. God gave back to Job everything he had lost. He also gave him sons and daughters. His daughters, Jemima, Keziah and Keren-happuch, were very beautiful. Job treated them just the same as their brothers.

God gave back everything Job had lost.

God is our Hope

Job's problem was solved after he prayed for his friends. Remember the people you should pray for. Ask God to bless them, forgive them and help them.

30. THE FIERY FURNACE

(DANIEL 3)

When Judah was defeated by Babylon many young men were taken captive. The best went to work in Nebuchadnezzar's palace. Three of these young men were Shadrach, Meshach and Abednego. They loved God and served him.

One day Nebuchadnezzar made a big gold statue in the plain of Dura which everyone had to fall down and worship. However, Shadrach, Meshach and Abednego would not do that. They loved the true God. Nebuchadnezzar threatened to throw them into a fiery furnace, but they said, "Our God is able to save us from this furnace. We will not serve your gods."

The king ordered that the fire be made seven times hotter. Shadrach, Meshach and Abednego were tied up and thrown into the flames. But the king was astonished when he saw not three in the fire, but four men walking around unharmed. "The form of the fourth is like the Son of God," he said. And when Shadrach, Meshach and Abednego came out of the fire not even a hair was singed. There wasn't even a smell of smoke on their clothes. Nebuchadnezzar then realised how powerful the one true God was.

God can save us.

God is True

The young men were brave in standing up for the truth. Ask God to make you brave enough to refuse to do something that is wrong.

31. DANIEL AND THE LIONS

(DANIEL 6)

Daniel was also taken captive to Babylon. Later on when King Darius came to power, Daniel was made chief adviser. The other officials were jealous. They tried to find fault with him, but he was honest and worked well. However, the officials knew that he prayed three times a day. They hatched a plot and approached the king. "You should issue a law, O King, saying that anyone who prays to any god or man except you in the next thirty days, should be thrown into the lions' den."

Darius was flattered and agreed. But when Daniel learned of the new law he knew he could not disobey God like that. Daniel went straight to his room and prayed to God. The officials saw this and immediately went to tell King Darius who became very upset. He did not want any harm to come to Daniel, but the law could not be changed. Daniel was thrown to the lions. "May your God, whom you always serve, rescue you," Darius told him.

That night Darius could not sleep. Next morning he hurried to the lions' den and called out to Daniel. How pleased he was to hear Daniel's voice. "My God sent his angel to shut the lions' mouths." God had kept Daniel safe.

Daniel went to his room and prayed to God.

God is our Refuge

Daniel was safe even in the lions' den because God was with him. Look up Psalm 4 verse 8. God keeps us safe too.

32. JONAH AND THE BIG FISH

(JONAH 1–4)

God told Jonah to go to Nineveh to preach to the wicked people there. But Jonah did not want to so he ran away to Joppa and boarded a ship heading for Tarshish. God then sent a violent and dangerous storm. The sailors were scared and when they discovered that Jonah was running away from God they were terrified. "Throw me overboard," said Jonah. "The storm is all my fault."

So the sailors threw Jonah into the stormy sea. The sea immediately became calm. The sailors saw God's power and worshipped him. But what happened to Jonah? Well, God sent a huge fish to swallow Jonah whole. This saved him from drowning. For three days and three nights Jonah lived inside the big fish. He prayed to God to forgive him and save him.

God made the fish vomit Jonah out on to dry land. Jonah had a second chance to obey God. This time he obeyed. He walked to the centre of Nineveh and preached to the people. "In forty days Nineveh will be destroyed because of sin." When the people heard this they repented. They were sorry for what they had done wrong. God had mercy and did not destroy the city.

Jonah was in the big fish.

God is Just

When Jonah disobeyed God it led to lots of trouble. If we do not obey God's Word that will cause trouble for us too.

33. JOHN THE BAPTIST

(LUKE 1)

Zacharias was a priest in God's temple. He was married to a woman called Elizabeth. They lived near Jerusalem and loved God. They were old and lived holy lives, but God had not given them any children.

One day when Zacharias was alone in the temple an angel appeared by the altar. "Don't be afraid," the angel said. "Your prayer has been heard. Elizabeth will have a son. You shall call his name John." The angel told him that the baby would bring joy to many. "I am too old," Zacharias protested, "and my wife is too old." The angel replied, "Because you do not believe me, you will be struck dumb until my words come true."

Soon Elizabeth was expecting a baby. She was delighted when he was born. Her friends and neighbours thought that the baby would be called after his father. His mother said, "No, he shall be called John." Zacharias wrote, "His name is John." Immediately he was able to speak again and he praised God. God the Holy Spirit had told him that John would be a preacher one day – warning people about sin and pointing them to the Lord Jesus Christ.

The angel said that the baby would bring joy.

God is Willing

Zacharias and Elizabeth waited a long time for a baby. When we pray God sometimes says, "Yes," sometimes "No," and sometimes "Wait". These are all good answers.

34. THE BIRTH OF JESUS

(MATTHEW 1–2)

Mary was a young Jewish woman who lived in the village of Nazareth. One day she had an amazing visitor. The angel Gabriel came and gave her a message from God. "You are going to have a baby boy. You will call him Jesus." Mary was afraid at first, but the angel told her that the baby was the Son of God.

Joseph was engaged to Mary. When he heard that Mary was expecting a baby, he was worried too. God sent Joseph a message in a dream. "Don't be afraid to take Mary as your wife. The baby is God's Son. You will call his name Jesus (which means Saviour) for he shall save his people from their sins." Joseph was happy to marry Mary then.

Later the Roman Emperor ordered everyone to go back to their home town to be enrolled. Mary and Joseph had to travel to Bethlehem (Joseph's home town) to be counted. Bethlehem was so busy. They could find no room at the inn. They had to find shelter where the animals were fed. That was where Jesus was born. Mary wrapped him in swaddling clothes and laid him in a manger for a cot.

Jesus shall save his people from their sins.

God is Wonderful

Look up John chapter 3 verse 16. God sent his Son to the world as a baby, so that those who believe in him would not perish, but have everlasting life.

35. SHEPHERDS, SIMEON AND ANNA

(LUKE 2)

Near Bethlehem, shepherds were out at night watching over their sheep. Suddenly an angel appeared and they were very afraid. "Don't be afraid," the angel said. "I bring good news for you and all people. Today a Saviour was born in Bethlehem – Christ the Lord. You will find the baby wrapped in swaddling clothes, lying in a manger." Then a crowd of angels praised God, "Glory to God in the highest. Peace and good will to all people." The shepherds hurried to Bethlehem and found Mary, Joseph and the baby just as the angel had said. They passed on the good news to everyone they met – praising God as they went back to work.

When the baby was eight days old he was given the name Jesus. Mary and Joseph took the baby to the temple to present him to God and to offer the sacrifice required by the law. A holy man called Simeon was thrilled to meet the special baby. "I am ready to die now," he said, "for I have seen God's salvation."

A godly old lady, Anna, lived in the temple and prayed all day long and at night too. She gave thanks to God when she met the baby Jesus.

The Shepherds hurried to Bethlehem

Jesus is Wonderful

The shepherds could not keep the good news to themselves. They spoke about him to all they met. We should tell others about Jesus too.

36. THE WISE MEN AND THEIR GIFTS

(MATTHEW 2)

Wise men from the east came to look for Jesus. They had seen a special star that told them the King of the Jews had been born. They went to look for him in Jerusalem, but did not find him there. King Herod was angry when he heard their story. His religious leaders told him, "The Messiah will be born in Bethlehem." So Herod sent the wise men there. "Come back and tell me when you have found him so that I can worship him too," he said. But he secretly meant to kill the child instead.

The wise men were guided by the star right to the house where Jesus was. When they saw the young child they worshipped him. They knew he was the Son of God. They gave him lovely presents of gold, frankincense and myrrh. But they did not go back to tell Herod where Jesus was. God warned them in a dream of Herod's evil plan and they went home another way.

God also warned Joseph. So in the middle of the night he took Mary and Jesus and travelled to Egypt. They stayed there until God's angel told Joseph it was safe to return. When they went back to Israel they settled in the village of Nazareth.

Wise men came to look for Jesus.

Jesus is to be Worshipped

You can worship Jesus too. The wise men worshipped Jesus and gave him gifts. We can also give him gifts – by loving him with all our heart, soul, strength and mind.

37. THE BOY JESUS

(LUKE 2 AND MARK 6)

Jesus grew up in Nazareth with his brothers and sisters. He was wise and good and always did what pleased God his Father. Every year Joseph and Mary went to Jerusalem to attend the Passover Feast. They took Jesus for the first time when he was twelve years old.

When it was time to go home, a large crowd travelled back to Nazareth. But the next day Mary and Joseph could not find Jesus. They had thought he was with someone else in the group. Quickly they hurried back to Jerusalem to look for him. After searching for three days, they found Jesus in the temple speaking with the teachers and asking questions. Everyone was amazed at his wise answers. Mary and Joseph were amazed too. Mary asked him, "Son, why did you treat us like this? Your father and I have been searching for you anxiously."

Jesus replied, "Why were you looking for me? Did you not know that I must be in my Father's house?" He meant the temple, the house of God. Jesus went back to Nazareth with Mary and Joseph. He was a good obedient son, becoming even wiser as he grew up. He worked as a carpenter, like Joseph.

Mary and Joseph could not find Jesus.

Jesus is Wise

Jesus learned about God his Father and the Scriptures. He discussed wise things with the teachers. We can read God's Word too and find out what God wants to tell us.

38. THE BAPTISM OF JESUS

(MATTHEW 3)

John the Baptist was a preacher, who told the people to turn from their sins. He lived a simple life in the desert of Judea. Many people from Judea and Jerusalem came to hear him preach. They confessed their sins, were truly sorry and turned from their sin to God. They were baptised by John in the River Jordan, which was a sign that they were having their sins washed away.

One day Jesus came to the River Jordan to see John. He asked John to baptise him. John was surprised. "I need to be baptised by you, but you are coming to me?"

Jesus persuaded him that this was the right thing to do. Jesus had no sin himself, but was baptised as an example to others, and to show us that although he was sinless and God, he was also fully man. So John baptised Jesus in the River Jordan. As he came out of the river, the heavens opened and the Spirit of God came down on him, looking like a dove. God the Father's voice spoke, "This is my Son whom I love, with him I am well pleased."

God was pleased with what Jesus had done.

John told people to turn from their sins.

God is Amazing

In Matthew 3 verses 16-17 we read about God the Father speaking from heaven, God the Son coming out of the River Jordan and God the Holy Spirit coming down looking like a dove.

39. JESUS IS TEMPTED BY SATAN

(MATTHEW 4)

Jesus was led by the Holy Spirit to the wilderness. He was there for forty days and did not eat any food. The devil came and tempted him to do wrong. He asked him to prove that he was the Son of God by turning stones into bread. Jesus did not do this. He replied to the devil with a verse from the Bible. "Man shall not live by bread alone, but by every word that comes from the mouth of God," (Deuteronomy 8:3).

The devil tried again. "Prove you are the Son of God and throw yourself off the temple roof. God says that his angels will help you." Jesus refused. Again he quoted God's Word. "Do not test the Lord your God," (Deuteronomy 6:16).

The devil tried a third time. He took Jesus to a high mountain and showed him the kingdoms of the world. "Worship me," he said "and I will give them all to you." Jesus refused and again quoted God's Word. "Worship the Lord your God and serve him only," (Deuteronomy 11:13). The devil then left Jesus. Angels came to attend to him. Jesus was tempted to sin, but he never gave in. He could not sin. He was God's perfect Son.

Worship the Lord your God and serve him only.

Jesus is Powerful

Jesus has power over sin and the devil and can help us when we are tempted to sin. Our sins can be forgiven by God through Jesus Christ. He defeated sin on the cross.

40. THE TWELVE DISCIPLES

(MARK 1–3)

As Jesus walked by the Sea of Galilee he saw two fishermen, Simon and his brother Andrew, throwing a net into the sea. "Come follow me," Jesus said, "and I will make you fishers of men." Instead of catching fish in a net, God would use them to draw people to himself. At once they left their nets and followed Jesus. Jesus gave Simon a new name – Peter, which means *a rock*. A little further on he met two other fishermen, James and his brother John. Jesus called them too. They left their father Zebedee in the boat with the hired men and followed Jesus.

Levi was a tax-collector. One day Jesus called him to follow. He obeyed and became a disciple too. His name was changed to Matthew. Jesus chose twelve men to be his special helpers – called disciples. Their names are Simon Peter, Andrew, James, John, Philip, Bartholomew, Thomas, Matthew another James, Thaddaeus, another Simon and Judas Iscariot. These men travelled about with Jesus. Their special job was telling the people the Good News about God.

"Come, follow me," Jesus said.

Jesus is Loving

Jesus loves his people. He died for them. He tells us to love one another. This will show others that we are his followers (John Chapter 13 verse 35). How can we show love to others?

41. THE MIRACLE AT THE WEDDING

(JOHN 2)

Jesus and his mother Mary were invited to a wedding in the town of Cana. Jesus' disciples were among the guests too. During the feast the servants discovered that the wine was finished. Mary told Jesus about the problem and she also told the servants, "Do whatever Jesus tells you."

In the room there were six big stone water pots. Each would hold 100 litres. "Fill these water pots with water," Jesus told the servants. They filled them up to the brim. "Draw out a cupful and take it to the man in charge of the feast."

The man drank some and called the bridegroom over. "This is good wine," he said. "People usually serve the good wine first. But you have kept the good wine till now."

The servants who had filled the waterpots with water knew that Jesus had performed a miracle. The water had been changed to wine. This was Jesus' first miracle. When his followers saw what had happened, they believed in him.

Jesus was invited to a wedding.

Jesus is the Miracle-worker

Jesus performed his first miracle when he changed water into wine. He still performs miracles when he changes the lives of the people who trust in him.

42. THE WOMAN AT THE WELL

(JOHN 4)

Jesus was in Samaria and sat down to rest by a well. The disciples went to buy food in a nearby town. Just then a woman came to draw water from the well and Jesus asked her for a drink. She was surprised that he spoke to her because Jews and Samaritans did not speak to each other. Jesus and the woman had a wonderful talk. "If you knew who asked you for a drink, you would have asked him and he would have given you living water," Jesus said. The woman did not really understand what Jesus was speaking about at first. He was not speaking about the water in the well, but about the real satisfaction that comes from loving and trusting in the Lord as Saviour.

Jesus told the woman that the way she was living was sinful. She realised that Jesus was special. Jesus pointed out to her how important it is to worship God from the heart. He told her that he was the promised Messiah, the Son of God and she believed in him. Quickly she left her water pot and ran to tell everyone, "Come and see a man who knows all about me. Is not this the Christ?" Many people believed because of what she said.

She left her water pot and ran to tell everyone.

Jesus is God and Man

The Lord Jesus was both God and man. Look up John chapter 4 verse 6 and 7. These verses show us that Jesus became tired and thirsty, like we do.

43. THE SOWER'S STORY

(MATTHEW 13)

Jesus told a story about a farmer and his field. "As the farmer sowed his seeds, some fell on the path. Birds ate these. Some fell on stony ground. The seeds grew quickly, but when the hot sun shone the shoots withered and died because the roots could not reach moisture. Other seeds fell among thorns and weeds which choked the good plant. But some seeds fell on good ground. These grew well and yielded a good harvest." The people enjoyed hearing this story, but not everyone understood it so Jesus explained the story or parable to his disciples.

The seed is like the Word of God. Some people hear God's Word, but the devil makes them forget it. That is like the seed on the pathway, stolen by birds. Other people hear God's Word and listen gladly. But when trouble comes, their interest withers away. They are like the seed on the shallow stony ground. The seeds sown in the thorns are like people who hear God's Word, but riches and pleasures choke their interest in the Bible. But some people hear the Word and love it and obey it. They are like the seed which fell on good ground.

Some seeds fell on good ground.

Jesus is our Teacher

Jesus told many parables or simple stories which made the lesson easier to remember. When you hear God's Word do you listen to it and obey it?

44. THE BUILDERS' STORY

(MATTHEW 7)

Jesus was a wonderful preacher and teacher. He often used stories of everyday happenings. These stories had hidden meanings about God and his kingdom. Only those who trusted and believed in God would understand their true meaning.

One story that Jesus told was about two men who each built a house for himself and his family. One man was wise. He built his house on a rock – the foundation was firm and strong. When the storm blew and the rain came battering down, the house was safe and solid. Jesus said that if we hear what God tells us in the Bible and put it into practice in our lives we are like the wise man. Our lives will be on a solid foundation and will stand up to the storms and difficulties of life.

The other man was foolish. He built his house on the sand. When the storm came, the foundation was washed away and the house collapsed. If we hear God's Word and do not obey it, we are like that foolish man. Our lives will be in ruins.

The wise man built his house on a rock

Jesus is Lord

God wants you to read his Word and obey what he tells you in his Word. One of the most important things he tells you to do is to "believe on the Lord Jesus Christ."

45. CALMING THE STORM

(MARK 4)

Jesus and the disciples set out to sail to the other side of the Lake of Galilee. Now this lake was sometimes a dangerous place to be. Violent storms could spring up suddenly out of nowhere. Huge waves would crash into the little fishing boats. While they were crossing the lake Jesus fell asleep on a pillow in the stern or back of the boat. But very soon a great storm blew up. The waves were so fierce and so high that the water came right over the sides of the boat.

The disciples were terrified, even though Jesus was with them. When the disciples could wait no longer they called out to Jesus to wake him up. "Lord, save us!" they shouted. "Do you not care that we are going to drown?"

Jesus got up and spoke to the wind and sea and said "Peace be still." The wind stopped blowing and the sea became calm. "Why were you so afraid?" he asked the disciples. "How weak your faith is." The disciples were amazed at Jesus' power over the wind and sea.

The waves came over the sides of the boat.

Jesus is God

Look up Psalm 107 verse 29. That tells us that God calms the storms and waves. What Jesus did was proof that he is God.

46. JESUS FEEDS A HUGE CROWD

(MATTHEW 14 AND JOHN 6)

Jesus and his disciples sailed across the lake to a quiet spot. Many people went to that place on foot, so when Jesus arrived, a crowd of over 5000 people wanted to hear him preach. Jesus took pity on them. He taught them and healed many sick people.

In the evening the disciples asked Jesus to send the people away to buy food. "Can you give them something to eat?" Jesus asked. Andrew spoke up. "There is a boy here who has five small loaves and two small fish. How could they feed so many people?" Jesus told the disciples to get the people to sit down on the grass. He then took the loaves and fish and gave thanks to God for them. Jesus broke them into pieces and handed these to the disciples who passed them round the huge crowd. Everyone had enough to eat.

Afterwards the disciples cleared up and collected twelve baskets of left over food. Jesus had provided more than enough. It was a miracle! Jesus the Creator of all food had made the five loaves and two fish enough to feed over 5000 people.

The boy had five loaves and two fish.

God is Powerful

A miracle is an extraordinary thing done by God's power. Jesus gave the people bread to eat. In John chapter 6 verse 35 we read that Jesus is the bread of life – the only really satisfying thing.

47. JAIRUS' DAUGHTER IS HEALED

(MARK 5)

Jairus was an important Jewish leader. When his twelve year old daughter became very ill, he begged Jesus to come and heal her. Jesus made his way towards Jairus' house, but there were crowds of people all around. Suddenly Jesus stopped and asked, "Who touched me?"

A nervous woman came out of the crowd and told him her story. "I have been ill for twelve years and spent all my money on doctor's bills. Nothing helped. When I saw you, Jesus, I thought I would just touch the hem of your garment and I could be healed. As soon as I touched I was healed."

Jesus encouraged the woman and then carried on to Jarius' house, but a servant hurried up to Jarius. "Your daughter is dead," he told him. When Jesus heard this he said, "Do not be afraid. Just believe and she will be made better."

When he arrived he took the young girl's hand and said, "Little girl, get up." Immediately she came back to life and got up out of bed. Her mother and father were overjoyed. "Give her something to eat," Jesus ordered.

"Give her something to eat," Jesus ordered.

Jesus is Mighty

Jesus showed his power over sickness and death. He helped a woman who had been ill for twelve years and a young girl who had been well for twelve years up till that day.

48. JESUS TEACHES ON A MOUNTAIN

(MATTHEW 5–7)

Jesus started to preach when he was about thirty years old. His first sermon was "Repent" - this means to be truly sorry for sin and turn away from it to God. One day Jesus preached a powerful sermon sitting on a mountain with his disciples around him. It is full of good advice about how to live. Jesus taught that in life – love is very important. It is not enough to love only those who are good to us. Jesus tells us to love those who are our enemies.

Jesus teaches about prayer. We should pray in a quiet, secret place, not trying to show off to other people. God knows what we need. He wants us to pray to him. If a little boy asked his father for bread, would he give him a stone? If the boy asked for a fish, the father would never give a serpent. So God in heaven gives good things to his children who pray to him.

Jesus warns us not to be critical of others. When we find fault with someone, we often have a bigger fault ourselves. Jesus said, "You tell your friend he has a speck of dust in his eye, when you have a big piece of wood in your own eye."

God knows what we need.

God is our Guide

Part of Jesus' sermon in Matthew chapter 5 is called *the Beatitudes*. He teaches us how to be truly happy. Remember that God in heaven gives his children good things.

49. MARTHA AND MARY

(LUKE 10 AND MARK 14)

Mary and her sister Martha lived with their brother Lazarus in the town of Bethany. They were good friends of Jesus. He sometimes went to their house for a meal. One supper time Martha was busy preparing a meal for Jesus. Her sister Mary was sitting quietly beside Jesus listening to all his wise teaching.

Martha was tired and cross because she had all the work to do. "Why don't you tell Mary to help me, Lord?" she demanded. "Don't you care that she has left me to do all the work alone?"

"Martha, Martha," replied Jesus lovingly. "You are anxious and bothered about lots of things. There is one thing that is most important. Mary is doing the right thing. What she has chosen will do her good always."

Sometime later Jesus was in Bethany for another meal. Martha was again busy helping to serve the food. Mary came with a very expensive jar of perfumed  ointment and poured it over Jesus' feet. She gave him her most precious possession. Some complained that this was a waste, but Jesus was pleased with her loving action.

Martha was busy helping to serve the meal.

Jesus is Patient

Do not be so busy that you do not have time to read or listen to the Bible. Martha was too busy, but Jesus told her this in a wise and loving way.

50. LAZARUS

(JOHN 11)

Martha and Mary were worried. Their brother Lazarus was ill. They sent for Jesus. Jesus heard, but did not rush to Bethany. When he did arrive Lazarus had been dead and buried for four days. Martha and Mary's house was full of friends who had come to comfort them. Martha ran out to meet Jesus, "If only you had been here," she said, "Lazarus would not have died."

"Your brother will rise again," Jesus assured her. Martha believed Jesus and walked calmly back home to tell her sister that Jesus wanted to see her. Mary went to tell Jesus of her sadness. Then they went to the place where Lazarus was buried. Jesus wept. "Take the stone away," Jesus ordered. They pushed the stone away from the opening to the grave. Jesus prayed to God the Father then shouted loudly, "Lazarus, come out!"

Lazarus walked out of the grave and Mary and Martha were overjoyed to have their brother brought back to life. Many people believed in Jesus, because they saw Jesus' power for themselves.

Lazarus walked out of the grave.

Jesus is Ready to Listen

When you feel sad tell the Lord Jesus all about it. He understands how we feel. He has felt sadness too. We can pray to him at any time. He is always ready to listen.

51. ZACCHAEUS

(LUKE 19)

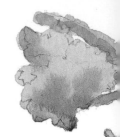

Crowds lined the streets of Jericho to see Jesus. Zacchaeus the tax collector was there. Nobody liked him. He was a cheat. He had made himself rich by charging people too much for their taxes. But he wanted to see Jesus too and because he was small he could not see over the heads of the people in front of him. However, he solved this problem by running along the road and climbing a sycamore tree to get a good view. When Jesus came to the sycamore tree he stopped and looked up at Zacchaeus. "Hurry down Zacchaeus," Jesus said. "I want to come to your house today."

Zacchaeus was delighted to welcome Jesus to his home. The people grumbled. They were not pleased that Jesus was a guest of Zacchaeus the cheat. However, meeting Jesus changed Zacchaeus' life. "Lord, I will give half of my money to the poor," he told Jesus. "If I have cheated anyone, I will give him back four times as much."

Jesus said, "Salvation has come to this house today. The Son of Man came to seek and to save the lost."

Zacchaeus climbed a tree.

Jesus is the Friend

Zacchaeus trusted in Jesus and his life changed. He did not have to become better before Jesus would speak to him. Jesus has come to save sinners. Read this in Luke 19 verse 10.

52. A LOST SHEEP AND A LOST COIN

(LUKE 15)

The religious leaders, called Pharisees, complained that Jesus was eating meals with sinners. Jesus explained that sinners were important to him. He told stories or parables about how God finds lost sinners. Those who believed in him would understand the meaning of these stories.

A man had a hundred sheep, but one went missing. He left the ninety-nine sheep and went to search for the lost one. He did not give up until he found it. He laid the lost sheep on his shoulders and went home happy. He called his friends over to celebrate. "Rejoice with me for I have found my lost sheep." In the same way there is joy in heaven every time God finds a lost sinner who repents.

A woman had ten precious coins, but lost one. She looked for it everywhere. She lit her lamp and swept all over the the house. When she found it she was delighted. She told her friends and neighbours. They were happy too. Jesus said that the angels in heaven are very happy when one lost sinner repents and is found by him.

She swept every corner of the house.

God is Ready to Forgive

There is joy in heaven when a sinner repents. To repent means to turn away from sin and to turn to God, being truly sorry for our sin. God is ready to forgive.

53. JESUS HEALS A BLIND MAN

(JOHN 9)

Jesus and his disciples met a man who had been blind since he was born. Jesus spat on the ground and made some mud with the saliva. He put the mud on the blind man's eyes. "Go and wash in the Pool of Siloam," he told him.

The blind man went and washed his eyes in the pool. Suddenly he could see. He had been healed by God's power. People were amazed. Some could not believe that it was him. The man said, "I am the man who was born blind. A man called Jesus put mud on my eyes, told me to wash in the pool, and now I can see."

"Where is this man?" they asked.

"I don't know" he replied. Jesus was no longer there.

The Pharisees found fault with Jesus and the man, but that man was delighted to receive his sight. "I was blind, but now I see!" he exclaimed.

 When he talked with Jesus again, he worshipped him as the Son of God. "Lord I believe," he said.

The blind man washed his eyes in the pool.

Jesus is Marvellous

The man was given two wonderful gifts. He was given sight and the grace to believe in Jesus Christ.

54. THE KIND MAN

(LUKE 10)

Jesus said that we should show love to our neighbour. A lawyer wanted to know who Jesus meant by a neighbour. So Jesus told a story about a man who was travelling on a dangerous road from Jerusalem to Jericho. Suddenly he was attacked by robbers and left beaten up on the roadside. A priest came along, but hurried on as fast as he could. Next came a Levite, also a religious man. He looked at the hurt man, but did not help. The next person to come along was a Samaritan. Jews and Samaritans did not usually speak to each other. But this one was sorry for the injured man. He gave him first aid, put him on his donkey, and took him to a nearby inn. He even stayed a night to look after him.

The next day the Samaritan gave some money to the inn keeper. "Look after this man. If you spend any more money on him, I will pay you next time I am passing."

"Who was the neighbour to the hurt man?" Jesus asked.

"The one who was kind to him," the lawyer replied.

"Go and be a good neighbour too," Jesus said.

He put him on a donkey. He took him to an inn.

God is Kind

It was surprising that the Samaritan man was the neighbour for the hurt man. Could you be kind and neighbourly to someone in a surprising way?

55. THE GOOD SHEPHERD

(JOHN 10)

Sheep know the voice of their shepherd and will follow him. Sheep will run away from strangers because they are afraid, but they trust their shepherd. Jesus calls himself the good shepherd. His people are the sheep. His people know his voice and will follow him. They are not afraid. They trust in him.

The shepherd makes sure that his sheep are safe. He is prepared to give his life to protect his sheep. Jesus the good shepherd gave his life for his people to make sure that they would be safe in heaven at last.

The shepherd knows his sheep and his sheep know him. Jesus, the good shepherd, knows his people and loves them. His people know and love him too. Jesus knows and loves his people so much that he gave his life for them.

David wrote many psalms and knew the Lord as a good shepherd. "The Lord is my Shepherd," he sang. "I shall not want. He leads me in green pastures and beside still waters."

The good shepherd leads his flock to food and refreshing water. Jesus, our Good Shepherd, leads us to nourishment and refreshment in his Word.

The shepherd knows his sheep.

Jesus is our Shepherd

The shepherd in Israel walked in front of his sheep and they followed his voice. Jesus wants us to follow him by listening to and obeying his Word – the Bible.

56. THE TAX COLLECTOR'S PRAYER

(LUKE 18)

Jesus told a story about two very different men who went to the temple to pray. One was a Pharisee, a very strict man. He thought he was always right and was very critical of other people. The other man was a tax collector. He had done many things that were wrong and he knew that. When the Pharisee prayed, he was proud of himself and thought he was very good. "God, I thank you that I am not greedy, dishonest or immoral like other people. I am not like that tax collector over there. I fast (go without food) twice a week and I give a tenth of my money to you." He was trusting in his own goodness to find favour with God. That was of no use.

The tax collector was different. He knew he was a sinner. He bowed his head and prayed. "God have mercy on me, a sinner." God heard and answered his prayer. The tax collector's prayer was humble. He was looking to God for forgiveness for his sin. He received forgiveness. The Pharisee did not see his need; he did not receive forgiveness.

We must see that we are sinners and ask God to show us mercy, like the tax collector did.

He prayed, "God have mercy on me a sinner."

God is Merciful

When you do wrong, ask God for forgiveness. He wants us to do this straight away. The Bible tells us that "whoever confesses and forsakes his sin, will have mercy," Proverbs 28 verse 13.

57. TO JERUSALEM

(MARK 11)

Jesus and his disciples set off for Jerusalem. When they reached the Mount of Olives, Jesus sent two of them to a nearby village. "You will find a donkey there. It has never been ridden before. Untie it and bring it to me. If anyone asks what you are doing, tell them that the Lord needs this donkey."

The two disciples found the donkey just as Jesus had said. When the owner asked what they were doing, they said, "The Lord needs it." The owner allowed them to take the donkey to Jesus. The disciples then put clothes on its back and Jesus rode the donkey into Jerusalem.

Crowds joined the procession. Some cut down palm branches and placed them on the road in front of Jesus. Others laid down their cloaks. They shouted out joyfully, "Hosanna! Blessed is the King who comes in the name of the Lord!"

Jesus rode into town hearing the shouts of praise and when he came to the temple he chased away the greedy men who were using the temple as a market place. Little children sang praise and cheered Jesus. He was delighted to hear them.

They found the donkey just as Jesus had said.

Jesus is the King of Kings

Jesus is the King of kings. His Kingdom is all who trust in him. A king rides to victory on a fine horse. Jesus just had a donkey, but he was victorious over sin at the cross.

58. THE LAST SUPPER

(LUKE 22 AND MATTHEW 26)

Every year God's people ate the Passover meal to remind them of how God saved them from slavery in Egypt. Jesus wanted to eat this meal with his disciples so he sent Peter and John to get it ready. "Follow the man carrying a water jar," said Jesus. "He will lead you to a house. The owner will show you a large upstairs room. Get everything ready there."

They followed Jesus' instructions and later Jesus and the others joined them. The Passover meal took on a new meaning that night. Jesus broke the bread and handed it round. "This is my body," he said. He passed round a cup of wine, "This is my blood. When you eat the bread and drink the wine, think of me."

We call this the Lord's Supper now. Followers of Jesus still remember his death in this way. Jesus asked his followers to do this until he came again. However one person in the upper room did not love the Lord. Jesus knew that Judas Iscariot would betray him. When he pointed this out, Judas Iscariot left the room. Jesus then spoke with his friends for many hours. They sang a psalm of praise before going to the Mount of Olives.

When you do this think of me.

Jesus is the Way to God the Father

The bread was broken and the wine was poured out. This is to remind us of Jesus' body being hurt and his blood being shed, when he died on the cross for sinners.

59. IN THE GARDEN OF GETHSEMANE

(MATTHEW 26)

Jesus and the disciples went to a garden called Gethsemane. "Sit here," he said "while I pray." He took Peter, James and John with him. "I am troubled," he said to them. "Stay here and keep me company."

Jesus went by himself to pray three different times. Each time Peter, James and John fell asleep. "Why are you sleeping?" he asked them. "Get up and pray." Just then Judas Iscariot appeared with a crowd of soldiers. They were all armed with swords and clubs. They had been sent by leading priests and elders.

Judas greeted Jesus with a kiss. This was not a sign of friendship, but a signal to show the soldiers which man was Jesus. The soldiers then grabbed Jesus to take him away. Peter lashed out with a sword and cut off the ear of the high priest's servant. "No more of this," said Jesus. He touched the man's ear and it was healed immediately. "These things are happening to make the Scriptures come true." The disciples ran away scared.

Jesus was arrested and taken to the high priest's palace.

Why are you sleeping? Get up and pray.

Jesus is Perfect

Judas was a bad man. He sold the sinless Lord Jesus to his enemies for thirty pieces of silver. Later he felt guilty, but he did not truly repent and turn back to God.

60. PETER DENIES JESUS

(MATTHEW 26)

Jesus was put on trial. People told lies about him to the judge. They mocked him and spat on him. Peter was in the courtyard. He sat down with the servants round a fire. He wanted to know what would happen to Jesus. A girl went to Peter and said, "Were you not one of those that went about with Jesus of Galilee?" Peter answered, "I do not know what you are talking about."

Then he went out to the porch and another girl saw him, and said to the people, "This fellow was with Jesus of Nazareth too." Peter denied this again, "I do not know the man."

After a short time a man said to Peter, "Surely you are one of Jesus' followers, for you speak like them." Peter spoke roughly, "I do not know the man."

Immediately the cock crew. Jesus turned round and looked at Peter. Peter remembered that Jesus had said to him the day before, "Before the cock crows, you will deny me three times." Peter was so sad. He went outside and cried bitterly.

Peter was so sad. He went outside and cried.

Jesus is Gracious

When Peter repented of his sin, Jesus forgave him. Later he became a brave preacher of the gospel. God still forgives sinners who repent. He can give us courage to face problems.

61. JESUS DIES

(MATTHEW 27, MARK 15)

Jesus was led away to be crucified. He would be nailed to a wooden cross and left to die. But he had to carry the cross on his back first. It was very heavy so they allowed him to get help from a man called Simon.

At Golgotha, a hill outside Jerusalem, they nailed Jesus to the cross and lifted it up. Jesus was not angry. He lovingly prayed to God, "Father forgive them, for they do not know what they are doing."

From twelve noon until three o'clock in the afternoon darkness was over the whole land. Jesus was bearing the punishment for all the sins of all his people. "Why have you left me alone?" he called out in agony to God. Then just before he died he called out strongly, "Father, into your hands I commit my spirit."

The big curtain in the temple was ripped in two. An earthquake split the rocks. Graves opened and the dead came back to life. These miraculous things amazed the soldiers. That evening a rich man called Joseph and his friend carefully took Jesus' body from the cross and placed it in a garden tomb. A big stone was put in front of the opening.

The curtain was ripped from top to bottom.

Jesus is Glorious

When the curtain was torn in two, it was a sign that Jesus had done something wonderful. Because of what he did on the cross, we can come straight to God to forgive our sins.

62. JESUS LIVES AGAIN

(JOHN 30 AND MARK 16)

Early on Sunday morning some women went to the tomb where Jesus was buried. They wanted to anoint the body with spices, but were worried about moving the huge stone. When they arrived they saw that the stone had already been moved away. Jesus' body was not there. An angel spoke to them. "You are looking for Jesus of Nazareth who was crucified. He has risen. He is not here. Tell his disciples and Peter that he will see them in Galilee."

Peter and John ran as fast as they could to the empty tomb where they saw the grave clothes neatly folded. They believed now what the women had told them. Mary Magdalene wept in the garden. She spoke to a man she thought was the gardener. The man spoke her name, "Mary." She knew that he was Jesus.

In the days that followed, Jesus appeared to all the disciples and to many other people too. Over 500 people saw the risen Lord Jesus. He came right into the room where the disciples were hiding. They were terrified, but he said to them, "Peace be with you."

Peter and John ran as fast as they could.

Jesus is Real

Thomas only believed it was Jesus when he saw the nail prints in Jesus' hand. We can't see Jesus like he did, but we should still believe in him. Those who do will be blessed.

63. PICNIC ON THE SHORE

(JOHN 21)

One evening Peter and some other disciples were at the Sea of Galilee. Peter was going fishing. The others decided to go with him. They fished all night, but caught nothing. When morning came they saw a man on the shore watching them. He asked them if they had any food. "No," they replied.

"Put your net down again on the right side of the boat and you will find some," he said. When they did that they caught a huge number of fish.

John then recognised Jesus. "It is the Lord," he said to Peter. Peter jumped into the sea to rush ashore. There, Jesus had a fire ready with fish already cooked and bread. Jesus said to them, "Bring the fish that you have just caught." Peter pulled the net ashore and they counted the catch; one hundred and fifty three big fish. Although there was such a big catch of fish the net was not broken.

"Come and have something to eat," Jesus said. He handed round the bread and fish and ate some himself.

Peter jumped into the sea.

Jesus is Alive

Jesus is alive today. We cannot see him with our eyes, but he answers prayers and changes lives. On the shore he ate bread and fish to show the disciples that he was human and alive!

64. JESUS GOES BACK TO HEAVEN

(LUKE 24 AND ACTS 1)

Jesus was seen by more than 500 people in the forty days that he was in the world, after he rose from the dead. When Jesus and his disciples went out of the city of Jerusalem to the Mount of Olives, Jesus told them that the Holy Spirit would come to them. "You will receive special power," he said. Jesus told them what he wanted them to do then. "You will tell the good news about me in Jerusalem and in all Judea and Samaria and the whole world."

Then he lifted up his hands to bless them and he was taken up into heaven right through the clouds. The disciples were astonished. They stood gazing up into the sky where Jesus had gone. Two angels in white clothes stood beside them. "Why are you staring up into heaven?" they asked. "You have seen Jesus being taken up into heaven. He will come back again one day the same way he left."

This filled the disciples with joy. They went back to Jerusalem ready to start the great work of preaching the gospel. They praised and worshipped God.

Tell the good news to the whole world.

Jesus is in Heaven

The Holy Spirit is God, equal in power and glory with God the Father and God the Son. Jesus is in heaven today and is sitting at the right hand of God.

65. THE DAY OF PENTECOST

(ACTS 2)

On the Day of Pentecost the disciples were together in a house. Suddenly there was a loud noise like a very strong wind. They all saw tongues of fire on each man's head. Then they were all able to speak in foreign languages. God the Holy Spirit had come and had given his power to help them preach the gospel to other nations. These men were given the special name, *apostle*.

Many foreigners visited Jerusalem. When they understood Peter and the others they were amazed. Each heard the gospel in his own language. Many were astonished by God's power, but some laughed and said, "They must be drunk."

Peter spoke to the crowd. "Listen to me," he said, "these men are not drunk. The Holy Spirit has come to them. Let me tell you about Jesus. He did many wonderful miracles. You cruelly killed him. But he rose from the dead."

The people were greatly affected by Peter's sermon and asked him what they

should do. Peter told them to "Repent and be baptised in the name of Jesus Christ." About 3000 people believed in the Lord Jesus Christ that day.

The Holy Spirit gave his power to each man.

God is Building His Church

A sinner believes in Christ because of God's work. No one decides to do it himself. Many came to Christ after Pentecost. "The Lord added to the church daily," Acts chapter 2 verse 47.

66. STEPHEN THE MARTYR

(ACTS 6–7)

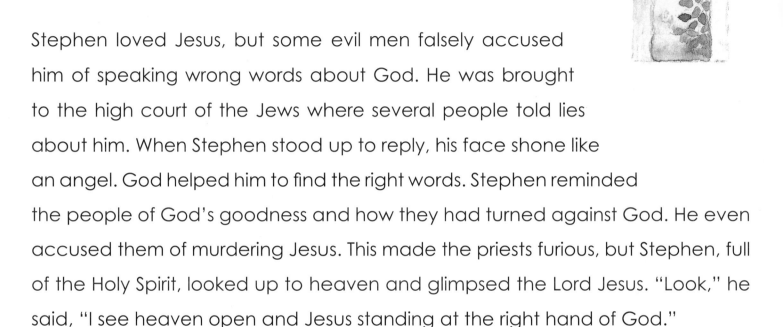

Stephen loved Jesus, but some evil men falsely accused him of speaking wrong words about God. He was brought to the high court of the Jews where several people told lies about him. When Stephen stood up to reply, his face shone like an angel. God helped him to find the right words. Stephen reminded the people of God's goodness and how they had turned against God. He even accused them of murdering Jesus. This made the priests furious, but Stephen, full of the Holy Spirit, looked up to heaven and glimpsed the Lord Jesus. "Look," he said, "I see heaven open and Jesus standing at the right hand of God."

The priests yelled and rushed at Stephen, dragging him out of the temple and out of the city. They picked up big stones and hurled them at him. Stephen prayed for himself and for the people who were killing him, "Lord Jesus, receive my spirit and do not hold this sin against them." He showed real Christian love to his enemies. A man named Saul was watching all that happened that day.

God helped Stephen to find the right words.

Jesus is the Lord of lords

Stephen was a martyr. He was killed because he trusted in Jesus. Pray for Christians today who suffer like this. Remember that Jesus is the Lord of lords. We can always trust him.

67. THE MIRACLE ON THE ROAD

(ACTS 9)

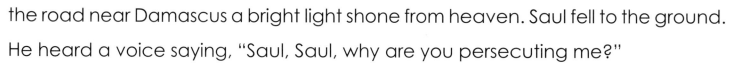

Saul was a strict, religious, man. He hated Christians and did all he could to hurt them. One day he travelled to Damascus to arrest followers of Jesus. On the road near Damascus a bright light shone from heaven. Saul fell to the ground. He heard a voice saying, "Saul, Saul, why are you persecuting me?"

"Who are you, Lord?" Saul asked.

"I am Jesus whom you are persecuting," came the reply. "It is dangerous for you to fight against me. Go to Damascus and you will be told what to do."

When Saul opened his eyes he was blind. This lasted for three days. He did not eat or drink anything. Then God sent Ananias to help him. Ananias was anxious about meeting Saul, but he did as God asked. "Brother Saul," he said, "the Lord Jesus who appeared to you on the road sent me to you, so that you may see again and be filled with the Holy Spirit."

Immediately Saul could see. He was baptised to show that he now believed in Jesus. He started telling others the good news about the Lord and his name was changed to Paul.

A bright light shone. Saul fell to the ground.

God is Free

Saul wrote to Timothy, "Jesus came to save sinners, of whom I am chief. But I was given mercy," 1 Timothy chapter 1 verse 15-16. We are sinners too and should ask God for mercy.

68. DORCAS AND HER SEWING BASKET

(ACTS 9)

Peter travelled around preaching the gospel and healing people. Many people believed in the Lord because of what they saw and heard.

A good lady called Dorcas lived in the town of Joppa. She loved the Lord Jesus. She served him by making clothes for poor children and their mothers. But one day Dorcas fell ill and died. Her friends were very upset. They heard that the apostle Peter was nearby. "Let's send for him," they said.

When Peter arrived at Dorcas' house, her friends were weeping in her room. They showed Peter the clothes that Dorcas had made for them. Peter told them all to leave the room. He kneeled down and prayed. He then turned to Dorcas and said, "Get up."

She opened her eyes and when she saw Peter she sat up. Peter took her hand and helped her out of bed. He called all her friends back. "Here is Dorcas, well again."

News of this wonderful happening spread through the town of Joppa and many believed on the Lord Jesus as a result.

Dorcas made clothes for poor children.

Jesus is Kind

Dorcas showed her love for Jesus by her kindness to poor families. She was a good neighbour like the man on page 114. Jesus is the most kind. His kindest act was to die for sinners.

69. PAUL THE MISSIONARY

(ACTS 13–14)

Paul became a missionary, travelling to many far-off places to tell others about Jesus who died for sinners. On his first trip he went with Barnabas and John Mark. They sailed to Cyprus to preach about Jesus. John Mark then left for home, but Paul and Barnabas went on to Asia, travelling through the land we now call Turkey. Many people heard the gospel preached and believed in Jesus. Others were jealous and wanted to get rid of Paul and Barnabas.

In Lystra a crippled man was healed when Paul spoke to him. The crowds were so impressed they began to worship Paul and Barnabas. This upset them very much. "We are just men like you," they exclaimed. "You should worship the living God who made heaven and earth and everything in it."

Then some Jews started to speak against Paul and Barnabas. The crowd who had been worshipping Paul now began to hurl stones at him. They dragged him outside the town and left him for dead. The believers came to help him. The next day Paul and Barnabas left for another town.

Worship the living God who made everything.

God is the One True God

God helped Paul. He can help us too. He wants us to be faithful to him. He is the only true God. In Exodus chapter 20 verse 3 he says, "You shall have no other gods before me."

70. PAUL TRAVELS AGAIN

(ACTS 16)

On his second trip Paul went with Silas and Timothy. Timothy had been taught the Bible when he was little by his mother and grandmother. God the Holy Spirit guided them to the sea port of Troas. That night Paul had a vision. A man begged him, "Come over to Macedonia and help us." Immediately Paul and his friends sailed to Macedonia in Europe. God wanted the gospel to be preached there.

At Philippi they stopped for several days. On the Sabbath they went to the river where some women were praying. One of the group, Lydia, was a business woman who sold beautiful cloth. She knew about God, but on that day the Lord opened her heart to respond quietly to the gospel message. She trusted in the Lord Jesus Christ. She and her family were baptised. Paul and his friends came to stay at her house.

On the way to the prayer meeting Paul met a slave girl who had made her owners rich by telling fortunes. God used Paul to deliver her from an evil spirit. She no longer told fortunes. Her masters were angry. They accused Paul and Silas of disturbing the peace, and they had them thrown in jail.

God opened Lydia's heart. She trusted Jesus.

God is Everywhere

Lydia and her friends met by the river to pray. They did not meet in a special building. We can pray to God anywhere – at home, at school, on a bus or in church.

71. THE PHILIPPIAN JAILER

(ACTS 16)

Paul and Silas were thrown into jail in Philippi. The jailer was told to guard them carefully. He put them into an inner cell and fastened their feet in the stocks. At midnight Paul and Silas were praying and singing praise to God in their prison cell. The other prisoners were listening to them. Suddenly a violent earthquake shook the foundations of the prison, the doors flew open and all the chains came loose.

The jailer woke up with a start. In a panic he grabbed his sword and was about to kill himself, as he was afraid that his prisoners had escaped. "Don't harm yourself," Paul shouted to him. "We are all here."

The jailer called for light and hurried to Paul and Silas. He asked a very important question. "Sirs, what must I do to be saved?"

"Believe in the Lord Jesus Christ and you will be saved," they told him. They then preached the Word of God to him and his family and household. They all believed and were baptised. The jailer washed Paul and Silas' wounds, took them home and gave them a good meal.

Believe in the Lord Jesus Christ.

Jesus is the Son of God

Pray that more people will hear the gospel. It is written "that you may believe that Jesus is the Christ, the Son of God, and that believing you may have life in his name," John chapter 20 verse 31.

72. PAUL'S LONG SERMON

(ACTS 20)

Paul stayed in Troas for a few days. On the first day of the week he met with local people for a service. As he was about to leave Troas the next day he had lots to say. Many gathered in an upstairs room and Paul spoke until midnight. A young man called Eutychus sat on an open window ledge, but began to feel very sleepy and slowly drifted off. Suddenly disaster struck! He fell to the ground three floors below. When the people reached him, he was dead. Paul put his arms around the young man and said, "Don't be afraid. He is alive."

Eutychus was restored to life. All the people went back upstairs again, shared bread together and Paul carried on speaking until dawn. He then left to continue his missionary journey which eventually took him back to Jerusalem. However, in Jerusalem he was arrested and put in prison. Evil men plotted to kill him, but his young nephew heard of the plot and warned him. Paul told his story to several important men, but no one wanted to deal with it. Then the decision was taken to send Paul to Rome where Caesar himself would hear his case.

The young man fell out the window.

Jesus is True

Paul met King Agrippa. He told him how Jesus had changed his life. Agrippa thought he was mad, but Paul said, "I speak the words of truth and reason," Acts chapter 26 verse 25.

73. JOURNEY TO ROME

(ACTS 27–28)

Paul's journey to Rome was full of adventures. In the Adriatic Sea his ship was tossed about in fierce winds. The crew threw cargo overboard to lighten the load. The storm was so fierce the sailors gave up hope of being saved. "Don't despair," Paul urged them. "Only the ship will be destroyed. An angel told me that all our lives will be spared. I have faith in God that it will happen as he told me."

After fourteen nights in the open sea the sailors sensed that they were nearing land. They took soundings and found that the sea was becoming shallower. They dropped four anchors from the stern and prayed for daylight. But Paul insisted that no one should leave the ship. He urged everyone to eat something. He gave thanks to God for the food. The others took courage from him and did the same.

At day break they saw a sandy beach. They all jumped overboard and either swam or floated to the shore on planks from the broken ship. All reached land safely on the island of Malta. Paul was there for three months before continuing to Rome.

The ship was in a very big storm.

God is Strong

When he was in danger, Paul had faith in God. He knew God would do the right thing. He had courage not because his faith was strong, but because his faith was in the strong God.

74. LETTERS TO THE CHURCHES

(EPHESIANS 6)

Paul wrote lots of letters sometimes called epistles – to the different churches that he had visited. They would have been read out when the church met together. These letters are part of our Bible today. In them Paul explains the truth about God the Father and the Lord Jesus Christ, and God the Holy Spirit. He puts right many of the mistakes that the Christian people were making. He gives lots of good advice about how to live in a way that is pleasing to God.

In one letter to the church at Ephesus, Paul told them how to fight against the evil schemes of the devil who would want to make them sin.

Paul gave the picture of a soldier dressed in his armour ready for battle. To fight against the devil the Christian must put on the whole armour of God – the belt of Truth, the breastplate of Righteousness, the shoes of the Gospel of Peace, the shield of Faith, the helmet of Salvation, the sword of the Spirit which is the Word of God and the battle cry of Prayer.

This armour protects the Christian and equips him to resist the devil.

Put on all the armour that God gives.

God is Good

Often Paul's letters start with a prayer. "Grace to you and peace from God our Father and the Lord Jesus Christ." Grace means mercy and forgiveness from God that we do not deserve.

75. THE PRISONER AT PATMOS

(REVELATION 1–22)

John wrote the book of Revelation when he was a prisoner on the island of Patmos in the Mediterranean Sea. Jesus sent an angel to John to give him a wonderful message. The angel showed John many amazing pictures. One was of heaven like a city of pure gold. The foundation of the city was made of precious jewels. The twelve gates were made of pearls. The street was of pure gold.

There was no temple in the city because the Lord Almighty and the Lamb (Jesus) are the temple. There was no need for the sun in the city. The glory of God was so bright that there was no darkness. A beautiful river flowed from the throne of God, shining like crystal. The tree of life was on each side of it, bearing twelve kinds of fruit. The leaves of the tree were for the healing of the nations. Nothing wicked will enter heaven, only those whose names are written in the Lamb's Book of Life – those who trust in the Lord Jesus.

Jesus said, "I am coming again very soon." John replied, "Amen, even so, come, Lord Jesus."

A beautiful river flowed from the throne of God.

God is Asking you to Come to Him

God the Holy Spirit and the church invite people to come to Jesus to save them from sin. They say, "Come. Let him who thirsts come, whoever desires, let him take the water of life freely," Revelation chapter 22 verse 17.

When you read this book to a child...

... remember that what you are reading is true. How you read God's Word to a child can have a lot to do with how well they understand the story or the message. So read with energy and enthusiasm - use your voice, facial features, even your actions to get across the meaning.

Story reading should be spontaneous but it is good to be prepared. Read the story yourself beforehand - think of different ways that you can bring it to life. Have your bible beside you as you prepare and as you read the story. Children may want to see for themselves where in the Bible the story is from. Preparation and a good Bible knowledge can only be a help as you read and explain God's Word.

Notice that in this book there are short sentences for the early reader to tackle by themselves or with a little help from you. We have attempted to give a variety to the reading level required in these individual sentences. So some words may be too difficult for a new reader but a child who has been reading for a year or two will enjoy the challenge of some new vocabulary.

Look at the Devotional Points. Focus on drawing closer to God. Learn more about God's character and the person of his Son, Jesus Christ. These sections will help you bring the message of the story into your daily life. Take advantage of your child's natural curiosity and investigate God's Word together.

Be prepared for questions. Teaching children can be a challenge but when you teach a child you will learn with them. If they ask a question that you don't know the answer to turn this to your advantage and make it into a learning game. If you know where to find the answer - go there, with your child. It may only be a trip to the nearest bookshelf or library. An older member of the family who has followed God and read his Word throughout their life is a valuable person to have around. If it is a biblical question looking up a bible dictionary will help and some bibles have indexes and useful information at the back of them. If your family attend church it may be a question that the child can ask a teacher or pastor.

If church is a new idea to you find out about churches in your area. When you find one that faithfully preaches God's Word this will be a great place to take your children. You will all be learning about God and worshipping him together.

In this big learning experience, use all the resources you have. Make reading the Bible the meaningful, mind expanding, life giving experience that it should be.

And every time before you open God's Word - pray together - that you will understand what God is telling you and that you will obey what he says.

Christian Focus Publications publishes books for adults and children under its four main imprints: Christian Focus, Christian Heritage, CF4K and Mentor. Our books reflect that God's Word is reliable and Jesus is the way to know him, and live for ever with him.

Our children's publication list includes a Sunday school curriculum that covers pre-school to early teens; puzzle and activity books. We also publish personal and family devotional titles, biographies and inspirational stories that children will love.

If you are looking for quality Bible teaching for children then we have an excellent range of Bible story and age specific theological books.

From pre-school to teenage fiction, we have it covered!

Find us at our web page: www.christianfocus.com

CF4•K